PROOF

OF THE

APOSTOLIC

PREACHING

PROOF

OF THE

APOSTOLIC

PREACHING

AN EARLY CHRISTIAN EXPOSITION
OF MESSIANIC PROPHECY

Irenaeus of Lyons

SERMON ⟨ON THE⟩ MOUNT
PUBLISHING

Cover design by Jonathan Lewis

ISBN 978-1-68001-038-1

For additional titles, contact:
Sermon on the Mount Publishing
P.O. Box 246
Manchester, MI 48158
(734) 428-0488
the-witness@sbcglobal.net
www.kingdomreading.com

Our Mission
To obey the commands of Christ and to teach men to do so.

First Printing—November 2023—1,500 copies

Introduction

If the prophets prophesied that the Son of God was to appear upon the earth, and prophesied also where on the earth and how and in what manner He should appear, and all these prophecies the Lord fulfilled, our faith in Him is well-founded, and the tradition of the preaching is true—that is, the testimony of the apostles.

—*Irenaeus*

The Book of Acts tells us that the Apostle Paul preached Christ in Jewish synagogues, demonstrating from the Old Testament Scriptures the truth of the message of Jesus' death, resurrection, and Messiahship (Acts 17:2–3; cf. Acts 18:28). The witness which the prophetic Scriptures give to the message of Christ is mentioned elsewhere in the New Testament as well (see, for example, Romans 1:2, 16:26; 1 Corinthians 15:3–4).

The apostles clearly knew about numerous prophecies of Christ in the Old Testament. It would be wonderful to have, from the pen of an apostle, an explanation of all the Old Testament prophecies which the apostles understood to refer to Christ. Sadly, no such writing exists. While we have scattered Old Testament quotations throughout the New Testament, there is no systematic explanation of messianic prophecy.

Thankfully, however, we do have the next-best thing: writings from early Christian authors, living near the time of the apostles, explaining how *they* saw Christ in the Old Testament.

The oldest of these writings is by Justin Martyr, a Samaritan who became a Christian and wrote several defenses of Christianity. One of these, titled *Dialogue with Trypho, a Jew*, is written in the form of a conversation between Justin and a Jewish man named Trypho. It gives detailed explanations of how the Old Testament foretold Jesus' life, ministry, death, and resurrection.

A slightly more recent writing, *Proof of the Apostolic Preaching* by Irenaeus of Lyons, is even more significant, because Irenaeus was himself only one human link removed from the apostles, and this gives his teachings added importance.

Who Was Irenaeus?

Irenaeus was a very important early Christian writer, but unfortunately, very little is known of his personal life. He spent his youth in Asia Minor, where he was a disciple of Polycarp, bishop of Smyrna. Polycarp had been a disciple of the Apostle John, and Smyrna was one of the two churches which Jesus had no criticism for in the letters to the churches in Revelation (see Revelation 2:8–11). Regarding the teaching he received from Polycarp, Irenaeus wrote:

> I listened to it all diligently, recording it not on papyrus, but in my heart. And by the grace of God, I always ruminate on them truly. . . .[1]

Polycarp met a martyr's death around AD 155. Irenaeus went to Gaul (now France), where he served the church as a presbyter. He was there during a time of intense persecution when many were martyred, and he undertook a journey to Rome to bring word of the persecution to the Roman church. Pothinus, the bishop in Lyons, Gaul, died at the age of ninety during the persecution, and Irenaeus succeeded him as bishop. Irenaeus probably died around AD 200.

---

1   Eusebius of Caesarea, *Church History* 5.20.7; Jeremy M. Schott, translator, *The History of the Church: A New Translation*. 2019. Oakland: University of California Press, 262.

WRITINGS

According to the church historian Eusebius, Irenaeus wrote several works, mostly dealing with defending the true faith against various heresies. Only two, however, have survived, and neither has survived intact in Greek, the language in which Irenaeus wrote.

The first of Irenaeus' works to survive is his large work, *Against Heresies*, in which he explained and defended orthodox Christianity and critiqued heretical groups, such as the Gnostics. While portions of the book survive in Greek, the complete work survives in a Latin translation.[2]

The second of Irenaeus' works to survive was long believed to be lost. Historians knew of its existence because Eusebius mentioned it. It was called *Proof* (or *Demonstration*) *of the Apostolic Preaching*. In 1904, a complete copy of an Armenian translation of the *Proof* was found—a major and exciting discovery. It was published for the first time in 1907 and has been published in translations into many languages since then. The first English translation was published in 1919.

IRENAEUS' AIMS

Irenaeus' aim in writing this work is well summarized in the quotation at the beginning of this introduction. If it could be shown that the Old Testament prophets had foretold the details of Jesus' life and ministry and the gospel which the apostles taught, then Christianity is well-founded and there is good reason to be confident that it is true. In contrast to *Against Heresies*, the *Proof* is not written as a polemic and rarely mentions opposing, non-orthodox opinions. Rather, it is written as a simple summary of salvation history and a guide to the prophetic Old Testament Scriptures, grounding its readers in the truths taught by the apostles and prophets.

---

2   A full English translation can be found in volume 1 of the *Ante-Nicene Fathers*.

Reading Irenaeus Today

Some aspects of Irenaeus' thought—and of early Christian thinking in general—seem unfamiliar or even strange to readers today. In this edition, explanations of early Christian concepts which may seem foreign to modern readers are briefly given in footnotes.

One area which will strike many readers as odd is Irenaeus' use of allegory in interpretation. In reading the Old Testament Scriptures, Irenaeus saw certain statements as prophecies of Christ by interpreting them allegorically. The Apostle Paul used the same method (see, for instance, Galatians 4:21–31), and many early Christian writers used the allegorical method of interpretation more freely than most Christians today are accustomed to.

Readers of Irenaeus will also note that many of his quotations of the Old Testament do not match what they read in their Bibles. This is because, like the New Testament writers normally did and all the other Greek-speaking early Christian writers did, Irenaeus quoted from the Septuagint. The Septuagint (abbreviated LXX) was the Greek translation of the Old Testament prepared by Jews in Egypt before the coming of Christ. It was used across the Greek-speaking Jewish world before Jesus' birth, and as Christianity spread across the Mediterranean world, it became the Old Testament of the early church as well.

In an age when all written materials were hand-copied, no two manuscripts of any work read exactly alike. Irenaeus' quotations occasionally differ even from the copies of the Septuagint which we have today. In those cases, this edition follows Irenaeus' quotation in the main text and points out the variant in a footnote.

About This Edition

This edition of Irenaeus' *Proof* is based on the translation by J. Armitage Robinson, originally published in 1920.[3] The language has been updated and the translation modified for smoother, easier reading. The translation was also compared with translations by Joseph

---

3   J. Armitage Robinson, translator, *St. Irenaeus: The Demonstration of the Apostolic Preaching*. New York: Macmillan. 1920. Digitized by Roger Pearse.

P. Smith[4] and Roger Behr,[5] and I have benefited from their work in modifying and annotating this version. All subheadings are added by the current publisher.

Unless otherwise noted, all Old Testament quotations in this work are quoted from the Lexham English Septuagint (LES). In some cases, Irenaeus bases his commentary on a textual variant not reflected in this translation. In those instances, the LES has been quoted, but modified to include the textual variant which Irenaeus was reading. These instances have been marked by footnotes. This edition does not, however, preserve every textual variant which Irenaeus (or his Armenian translator) uses. For further information on textual details, see the thorough notes in the translations of Smith and Behr.

Since the Psalms are numbered differently in the Masoretic Text and the Septuagint, references to the Psalms give both numbers. All New Testament quotations are taken from the King James Version.

Near the close of the work, Irenaeus writes: "This is the way of life which the prophets proclaimed, Christ established, the apostles delivered, and the Church in all the world hands on to her children. This must we keep with all certainty, with a sound will and pleasing to God, with good works and a right-willed disposition."

As you read, may you be blessed and may your faith in the truth of the apostles' gospel be strengthened.

—*Andrew V. Ste. Marie*
May 2023

---

4   Joseph P. Smith, translator, *Proof of the Apostolic Preaching*. Mahwah: Paulist Press, 1978.
5   Roger Behr, translator, *On the Apostolic Preaching*. Crestwood: St. Vladimir's Seminary Press, 1997.

Proof of the Apostolic Preaching

I know, my beloved Marcianus, your desire to walk in godliness, which alone leads man to eternal life. I rejoice with you and pray that you may preserve your faith entire and be pleasing to God who made you. If only it were possible for us to be always together, to help each other and to lighten the labor of our earthly life by continual discourse on profitable things! Although we are now parted from one another, yet according to our ability we will not fail to speak with you a little by writing, and to briefly show the preaching of the truth for the confirmation of your faith.

We send you as it were a manual of essentials, that little by little you may attain to much, learning in a short space all the members of the body of truth, and receiving in brief the demonstration of the things of God. It shall be fruitful to your own salvation, and you shall put to shame all who promote falsehood, and bring with all confidence our sound and pure teaching to everyone who desires to understand it.

There is one way leading upwards for all who see, illuminated with heavenly light, but many, dark, and contrary are the ways of those who see not. The upward way leads to the kingdom of heaven, uniting man to God; but those dark ways carry one down to death, separating man from God. Therefore, it is needful for you and for all who care for their salvation to make your course unswerving, firm, and sure by means of faith. Falter not, nor be detained by material desires, nor turn aside and wander from what is right.

Man is a living being, made of soul and flesh. He must exist by both of these, and from both of them offences come. But purity of the flesh is the denying of all shameful things and all unrighteous deeds. And purity of the soul is keeping faith towards God entire, neither adding to nor diminishing from it.

For godliness is obscured and dulled by the soiling and the staining of the flesh. Godliness becomes no longer whole if falsehood enters into the soul. However, godliness remains in its beauty and in its measure when truth is constant in the soul and purity constant in the flesh. For what profit is it to know the truth in words, and to stain the flesh with works of evil? Or what profit can purity of the flesh bring, if truth is not in the soul? For purity and truth rejoice with one another, and are allied to bring man face to face with God. Wherefore the Holy Spirit says through David: "Blessed is the man who does not go in the counsel of the ungodly":[1] that is, the counsel of the heathen. Ungodly men do not worship the God who truly exists. And therefore the Word says to Moses: "I am the One who exists":[2] but the ungodly do not worship the God who is. "And does not stand in the way of sinners":[3] but sinners are those who know about God and yet do not keep His commandments; that is, disdainful scorners. "And does not sit in the seat of evil persons":[4] now the evil are those who by wicked and perverse doctrines corrupt not only themselves, but others also. For the seat is a symbol of teaching. All heretics are like this: they sit in the seats of the evil persons, and those who receive the venom of their doctrine are corrupted.

Now, that we may not suffer such an outcome, we must hold the rule of the faith without deviation, and do the commandments of God, fearing Him as Lord and loving Him as Father. That comes by faith, for Isaiah says: "If you do not trust, neither will you under-

---

1   Psalm 1:1.
2   Exodus 3:14.
3   Psalm 1:1.
4   Ibid.

stand."[5] And faith is produced by the truth, for faith rests on things that truly are. For we believe in things that are, as they are. Believing in things that are, as they ever are, we keep firm our confidence in them. Since faith is the perpetuation of our salvation, we must take much pains to maintain it, so that we may have a true comprehension of the things that are.

Now faith does this for us, even as the Elders, the disciples of the apostles, have handed down to us. First, it reminds us that we have received baptism for the remission of sins, in the name of God the Father, and in the name of Jesus Christ, the Son of God, who was incarnate and died and rose again, and in the Holy Spirit of God. This baptism is the seal of eternal life, and is the new birth unto God, that we should no longer be the sons of mortal men, but of the eternal and perpetual God. The everlasting and continuing [One] is God, and is over all things that are made, and all things are put under Him; and all the things that are put under Him are His own. For God is not ruler and Lord over someone else's things, but over His own; and all things are God's, and therefore God is Almighty, and all things are of God.

The things that exist have their beginning from some great cause; and the beginning of all things is God. For He Himself was not made by any; rather, by Him all things were made. Therefore it is right to believe that there is One God, the Father, who made and fashioned all things from nothing, and who, containing all things, is alone uncontained. Now among "all things" is this world of ours, and in the world is man; so then this world also was formed by God.

Thus there is shown forth One God, the Father, not made, invisible, Creator of all things, above whom there is no other God, and after whom there is no other God. And, since God is rational, therefore by the Word[6] He created the things that were made. God is Spirit, and by the Spirit He adorned all things; as also the prophet

---

5   Isaiah 7:9.
6   The Greek word *Logos*, used in the Gospel of John and in the early Christian writings to refer to Christ, means both "word" and "reason" in Greek. The English word "logic" comes from a related Greek word. Thus, when the early Christians thought of Christ as *Logos*, they understood Him to be both the Word and the Reason of the Unbegotten Father.

says: "By the word of the Lord the heavens were made firm, and by the spirit of his mouth, all their power."[7] As the Word establishes, giving body and granting the reality of being, the Spirit gives order and form to the diversity of the powers. Then rightly and fittingly is the Word called the Son, and the Spirit the Wisdom of God. Rightly does Paul, His apostle, say: "One God and Father of all, who is above all, and through all, and in you all."[8] "Above all" is the Father, and "through all" is the Son. Through the Son, the Father made all things. "In you all" is the Spirit, who cries, "Abba Father,"[9] and fashions us into the likeness of God. Now the Spirit shows forth the Word, and therefore the prophets announced the Son of God; and the Word utters the Spirit, and therefore is Himself the announcer of the prophets, and leads and draws us to the Father.

THE RULE OF FAITH

This then is the rule of our faith.[10] This is the foundation of the building, the stability of our lives: God, the Father, not made, not material, invisible; one God, the Creator of all things; this is the first article of our faith.

The second article is: the Word of God, the Son of God, Christ Jesus our Lord, who was revealed to the prophets through their prophesying and according to the direction of the Father. Through Him all things were made, and at the end of the times He will complete and gather up all things. He was made man among men, visible and tangible, in order to abolish death, show forth life, and produce a community of union between God and man.

And the third article is this: the Holy Spirit, through whom the prophets prophesied, and the fathers learned the things of God. The Holy Spirit, who led the righteous forth into the way of righteous-

---

7   Psalm 33 (32 LXX):6.
8   Ephesians 4:6.
9   Galatians 4:6.
10   In early Christianity, the rule (Greek *kanon*) of faith was the standard doctrinal statement which defined orthodoxy. While there was not one definitive version of the rule of faith across the whole church, versions preserved in various early Christian writings were all very similar. The Apostles' Creed is one such example.

ness and was poured out in the end of times in a new way upon mankind in all the earth, renewing man unto God.

The baptism of our regeneration proceeds through these three points: God the Father bestowing on us regeneration through His Son by the Holy Spirit. For all who have the Spirit of God are led to the Word, that is, to the Son; and the Son brings them to the Father; and the Father causes them to possess incorruption. Without the Spirit it is not possible to behold the Word of God, and without the Son no one can draw near to the Father; for the knowledge of the Father is the Son, and the knowledge of the Son of God is through the Holy Spirit; and, according to the good pleasure of the Father, the Son ministers and dispenses the Spirit to whomsoever the Father wills and as He wills.

WHO THE FATHER IS

By the Spirit the Father is called the Most High, the Almighty, and the Lord of Hosts, that we may learn that God is Creator of heaven, earth, and all the world, of angels and men. As Lord of all, through Him all things exist and by Him all things are sustained. He is merciful, compassionate, and very tender, good, just, and God of all, Jews and Gentiles alike, and of them that believe. To those who believe He is a Father, for in the end of the times He opened up the covenant of adoption.

To the Jews He was known as Lord and Lawgiver, for in the intermediate times, when man forgot God and departed and revolted from Him, He brought them into subjection by the Law. He did this so that they might learn that they had as Lord the Maker and Creator, who also gives the breath of life, and whom we ought to worship day and night. To the Gentiles He was known as Maker and Creator and Almighty; to all men, as Sustainer and Nourisher and King and Judge. For none shall escape and be delivered from His judgment, neither Jew nor Gentile, nor believer that has sinned, nor angel. Those who now reject His goodness shall know His power in judgment, according to that which the blessed apostle says: "Not knowing that the goodness of God leadeth thee to repentance; but after thy hardness and impenitent heart treasurest up unto thyself wrath against the day of wrath and revelation of the righteous judgment of God; Who will render to every man according to his deeds."[11] This is He who is called in the Law the God of Abraham, the God of Isaac, and the God of Jacob, the God of the living. And yet the sublimity and greatness of this God is unspeakable.

Now this world is encompassed by seven heavens,[12] in which dwell powers and angels and archangels, serving God, the Almighty and Maker of all things—not as though He was in need, but that they may not be idle and ineffectual. Wherefore also the Spirit of God is manifold in His indwelling, and the prophet Isaiah reckons that He gave seven forms of service when He rested on the Son of God, that is the Word, when He came as man. "And God's spirit," he says, "will rest on him, a spirit of wisdom and intelligence, a spirit of counsel and strength, a spirit of knowledge and piety. He will fill him with a spirit of the fear of God."[13] Now the heaven which is first from above,[14] and encompasses the rest, is that of wisdom; and the second from it, of understanding; and the third, of counsel; and the fourth, reckoned from above, is that of might; and the fifth, of knowledge; and the sixth, of godliness; and the seventh, this firmament of ours, is full of the fear of this Spirit which gives light to the heavens. For, as the pattern of this, Moses received the seven-branched candlestick that shone continually in the holy place; for as a pattern of the heavens he received this service, according to that which the Word spoke to him: "See that you make everything according to the pattern shown to you on the mountain."[15]

Now this God is glorified by His Word, who is His Son, and by the Holy Spirit, who is the Wisdom of the Father of all. He is glorified by the powers of the Word and Wisdom, which are called

---

11 Romans 2:4–6 (punctuation modified).
12 Though not found in the Bible, the idea of seven heavens is found in some Second Temple-era Jewish works. It may also have been held by other early Christians. Irenaeus relates the seven heavens to the seven powers of God's Spirit given to Christ in Isaiah 11.
13 Isaiah 11:2–3a.
14 That is, beginning at the highest heaven.
15 Exodus 25:40.

Cherubim and Seraphim, which glorify God with unceasing voices, and every created thing that is in the heavens offers glory to God the Father of all. By His Word He created the whole world, and in the world are the angels; and to all the world He has given laws wherein each thing should abide, so that each would fulfill his appointed task and not overstep their boundaries determined by God.

The Word in the Garden

But God has formed man with His own hands, taking from the earth that which was purest and finest, and mingling in measure His own power. He traced His own form on man, so that which should be seen should be of divine form, for man was formed and set on the earth as the image of God. And so that he might become living, God breathed on his face the breath of life, so that man should be like God both in breath and in form. Moreover, man was free and self-controlled, being made by God for this end, that he might rule all those things that were upon the earth. And this great created world, prepared by God before the creation of man, was given to man as his place. In this place were also the servants of that God who formed all things; and the steward, who was set over all his fellow-servants. Now the servants were angels, and the steward was the archangel.

Now, having made man as lord of the earth and all things in it, God secretly appointed him lord also of those who were servants in it. They, however, were in their perfection; but the lord, that is, man, was but small; for he was a child, and it was necessary that he should grow, and so come to perfection. And, that he might have nourishment and grow, with festive and dainty food, God prepared him a place better than this [present] world, excelling in air, beauty, light, food, plants, fruit, water, and all other necessities of life, and its name is Paradise. This Paradise was so fair and good that the Word of God continually resorted thither, and walked and talked with the man, foreshadowing what should occur in the future, namely that He should dwell and talk and be with men, teaching them righteousness. But man was a child, not yet having his understanding perfected. Because of this, he was easily led astray by the deceiver.

While man lived in Paradise, God brought before him all living things and commanded him to give names to them all, "and anything, whatever Adam named it as a living soul, this was its name."[16] And He determined also to make a helper for the man; for God said, "It is not good that the human is alone; let us make for him a helper like him."[17] For among all the other living things there was not found a helper equal and comparable and similar to Adam. But God Himself "laid a trance upon Adam and put him to sleep;"[18] and so one work might be accomplished from another, since there was no sleep in Paradise, this was brought upon Adam by the will of God; and God "took one of his ribs and filled up the flesh in the place of it. The Lord God built the rib that he took from Adam into a woman, and he led her to Adam."[19] Seeing her, he said, "Now this is bone from my bones and flesh from my flesh; she will be named 'Woman' because she was taken from her man."[20]

And Adam and Eve—for that is the name of the woman—"were naked . . . and they did not feel shame,"[21] for they had innocent and childlike minds, and it was not possible for them to imagine and understand anything of the wickedness which is born in the soul through lusts and shameful desires. For they were at that time whole, preserving their original nature; since they had the breath of life which was breathed on them at their creation, and while this breath remains in its place and power, it has no comprehension and understanding of things that are vulgar. Therefore they were not ashamed, kissing and embracing each other in purity like children.

---

16 Genesis 2:19.
17 Genesis 2:18.
18 Genesis 2:21.
19 Genesis 2:21b–22.
20 Genesis 2:23.
21 Genesis 2:25 (3:1 LXX).

MAN DEPARTS FROM GOD'S CREATED INTENT

God did not intend that man would conceive thoughts too high, and be exalted and uplifted, as though he had no lord, because of the authority and freedom granted to him, and so should transgress against his Maker, God. Nor did God intend for man to overstep his measure, and entertain selfish pride in opposition to God. Therefore God gave him a law so that he might recognize that the Lord of all was his lord. God gave him certain rules, so that, if he should keep the commandment of God, he would forever remain as he was, immortal. But if he would not keep it, he should become mortal and be dissolved to the earth from where his body had been taken. Now the commandment was this: "From every tree that is in the paradise you may eat for food, but from the tree for knowing good and evil, you will not eat from it. And on whichever day you eat from it, you will surely die."[22]

The man did not keep this commandment, but was disobedient to God, being led astray by the wicked angel who was envious of man because of the great gifts of God which He had given to him. He both brought himself to nothing and made man sinful, persuading him to disobey the commandment of God. So the angel, becoming by his falsehood the author and originator of sin, himself was struck down, having sinned against God, and caused the man to be cast out from Paradise. And, because by the prompting of his own disposition he apostatized and departed from God, he was called in Hebrew *Satan*, that is, *Apostate*[23]; but he is also called Slanderer. Now God cursed the serpent which carried and conveyed the Slanderer; and this curse came on the beast himself and on the angel hidden and concealed in him, even on Satan. Then God put man away from His presence, removing him and making him to dwell on the way to Paradise at that time, because Paradise does not receive the sinful.

Being barred from Paradise, Adam and his wife, Eve, fell into many troubles of anxious grief, going about with sorrow and toil and

22 Genesis 2:16b–17.
23 "Satan" actually derives from the Hebrew for "adversary" or "opposer."

lamentation in this world. For under the beams of this sun man tilled the earth, and it put forth thorns and thistles, the punishment of sin. Then was fulfilled that which was written: "And Adam knew Eve, his wife, and she conceived and brought forth Cain;"[24] and after him "she proceeded to bring forth his brother, Abel."[25] Now the apostate angel, who led man into disobedience, made him sinful, and caused his expulsion from Paradise, was not content with the first evil. Therefore he wrought a second on the brothers. Filling Cain with his spirit, he made him a murderer of his brother. And so Abel died, slain by his brother; signifying that from then on some would be persecuted and oppressed and slain, the unrighteous slaying and persecuting the righteous. At this, God was angered yet more, and cursed Cain. It came to pass that everyone of that race in successive generations was made like to the begetter. And God "raised up" another son to Adam, "in the place of Abel"[26] who was slain.

WICKEDNESS SPREADS

And then for a very long while, wickedness extended and spread. It reached and laid hold upon the whole race of mankind, until only a very small group of righteous remained among them. Illicit unions took place upon the earth, since angels were united with the daughters of mankind, and they bore to them sons who were called giants for their exceeding greatness.[27] And the angels brought as presents to their wives teachings of wickedness, in that they taught them the uses of roots and herbs, dyeing in colors and cosmetics, the discovery of rare substances, love-potions, hatreds, loves, concupiscence, constraints of love, spells of witchcraft, and all sorcery and idolatry hateful to God.[28] By the entry of these things into the world, evil spread and righteousness diminished and was weakened.

---

24 Genesis 4:1.
25 Genesis 4:2.
26 Genesis 4:25.
27 Genesis 6:1–4. The early Christians as well as Second-Temple Jews understood the "sons of God" in this passage to be fallen angelic beings who cohabited with human women, producing giant offspring.
28 This passage paraphrases the account as told in the book of 1 Enoch 6–8. This pseudepigraphal book, purporting to be written by the patriarch Enoch, was composed early in the Second Temple

[This continued] until God judged the world by means of a flood, in the tenth generation from the first-formed [man]. Noah alone was found righteous. He, being righteous, was delivered, with his wife and his three sons, and the three wives of his sons, being shut up in the ark with the animals which God had commanded Noah to bring into the ark. And when destruction came upon all humans and animals on earth, those in the ark escaped. Now the three sons of Noah were Shem, Ham, and Japheth. By them the race was multiplied; for they were the beginning of mankind after the Flood.

Now one of them was cursed, while the two [others] inherited a blessing by reason of their works. For the younger of them, who was called Ham, having mocked his father, was therefore condemned because of his impiety and unrighteousness against his father. He received a curse; and all his posterity were also involved in the curse; for his descendants were accursed, and in sins they increased and multiplied. But Shem and Japheth, his brothers, because of their piety towards their father, obtained a blessing. Now the curse Ham received from his father Noah is this: "Cursed be Ham the child;[29] A household servant he will be to his brothers."[30] This curse having come upon his race, his many descendants upon the earth, [even] for fourteen generations, grew up in a wild condition. Then they were cut off by God, being delivered up to judgment. For the Canaanites, Hittites, Perezites, Hivites, Amorites, Jebusites, Gergasites, and the Sodomites, as well as the Arabians, the dwellers in Phoenicia, all the Egyptians, and the Libyans, are Ham's posterity, and have fallen under the curse; for the curse lasts long over the ungodly.

And so the curse was passed on. But the blessing passed on to the race of him who was blessed, to each in his own order. For first Shem

period. It describes the "sons of God," the angelic lovers of human women, as introducing magical arts, cosmetics, and the production of weapons, as well as other skills, to humanity. This book is represented among the Dead Sea Scrolls.

29 Irenaeus' copy of the Septuagint apparently read this way, rather than having Noah curse "the child of Ham," Canaan.

30 Genesis 9:25. Modified from Lexham English Septuagint.

was blessed in these words: "Blessed be the Lord the God of Shem, and Ham[31] will be his servant."[32]

The power of the blessing is this, that the God and Lord of all should be to Shem a peculiar possession of worship. And the blessing extended unto Abraham, who was in the tenth generation from Shem. Therefore the Father and God of all was pleased to be called the God of Abraham, the God of Isaac, and the God of Jacob, because the blessing of Shem reached out and attached itself to Abraham. Now the blessing of Japheth is as follows: "May God make room for Japheth. Let him dwell in the houses of Shem, and let Ham[33] become their servant."[34] That is to say: in the end of the ages he blossomed forth, at the appearing of the Lord, through the calling of the Gentiles, when God enlarged unto them the calling; and "into all the earth their voice went out, and their words into the ends of the inhabited world."[35] The enlarging, then, is the calling from among the Gentiles, that is to say, the Church. "Let him dwell in the houses of Shem,"[36] that is, in the inheritance of the fathers, receiving in Christ Jesus the right of the firstborn. So in the rank with which each was blessed, in that same order through his posterity he received the fruit of the blessing.

A NEW RACE OF MEN
Now after the Flood, God made a covenant with the whole world, even with every living thing of animals and of men, that He would not again destroy all that grew upon the earth with a flood. And He gave them this sign: "At the time when I collect clouds on the earth, my rainbow will be seen in the cloud, and I will remember my covenant . . . and the water no longer will become a flood, so as to wipe out all flesh."[37] And He changed the food of men, giving them

---

31 Irenaeus' copy again reads "Ham" rather than "Canaan."
32 Genesis 9:26. Modified from Lexham English Septuagint.
33 Irenaeus' copy again reads "Ham" rather than "Canaan."
34 Genesis 9:27. Modified from Lexham English Septuagint.
35 Psalm 19:4 (18:5 LXX).
36 Genesis 9:27.
37 Genesis 9:14–15.

permission to eat flesh: for from Adam until the Flood, men ate only of seeds and the fruit of trees, and to eat flesh was not permitted to them. But since the three sons of Noah were the beginning of a race of men, God blessed them for multiplication and increase, saying:

> Increase and multiply and fill the earth and exercise dominion over it. And the trembling and fear of you will be upon all the wild animals of the earth and on all the birds of the heavens and on all the moving things on the earth and all the fish of the sea. . . . And every moving thing that is living will be yours for food; like grassy vegetables, I give you all things. But you shall not eat meat with the blood of life. For indeed, I will seek out your life blood, I will seek it at the hand of all the wild animals, and I will seek the life of the human at the hand of a fellow human. One who sheds the blood of a human shall be shed in place of his blood.[38]

For God made man in His image; and the image of God is the Son, after whose image man was made; and for this cause He appeared in the end of the times that He might show the image [to be] like unto Himself. According to this covenant the race of man multiplied, springing up from the seed of the three. "And all the earth was one language."[39]

And they arose and came from the land of the east; and, as they went through the land, they chanced upon the land of Shinar, which was broad; and there they undertook to build a tower. They sought means to go up to heaven, and to be able to leave their work behind as a memorial to those men who should come after them. Their building was made with burnt bricks and bitumen; and the boldness of their audacity went forward, as they were all of one mind and consent, and by means of one speech they served the purpose of their desires. But so that the work should advance no further, God divided their tongues, that they should no longer be able to understand each other. So they were scattered, and took possession of the world, and lived in groups and companies each according to his language; thus the diverse tribes and various languages upon the earth originated. So then three races of men took possession of the earth. One of

---

38 Genesis 9:1b–6a.
39 Genesis 11:1.

them was under the curse, and two under the blessing. The blessing first of all came to Shem, whose race dwelt in the east and held the land of the Chaldeans.

ABRAHAM SEEKS GOD

In the tenth generation after the Flood, Abraham appeared, seeking for the God who by the blessing of his ancestor was due and proper to him. And when, urged by the eagerness of his spirit, he went all about the world, searching for God, and failing to find Him, God took pity on him and appeared unto Abraham, making Himself known by the Word, as by a beam of light. For He spoke with him from heaven, and said unto him: "Go out from your land and from your kinsfolk and from the house of your father into whatever land I will show to you,"[40] and dwell there. Abraham believed the heavenly voice. Being then of ripe age, even seventy years old, and having a wife, he went forth from Mesopotamia, taking with him Lot, the son of his deceased brother. And he came into the land which now is called Judaea, where there lived seven tribes descended from Ham. There God appeared unto him in a vision and said: "I will give you and your offspring all the land that you see, forever."[41] God further told him that his descendants would be strangers in a land not their own, and be ill-treated there, being afflicted and in bondage for four hundred years. But in the fourth generation, they would be delivered and return to the place that was promised to Abraham, and God would judge the nation that had brought his descendants into bondage.

Then, that Abraham might know the multitude as well as the glory of his descendants, God brought him out at night, and said: "Look up now to the heavens and count the stars, if you can count them. . . . Your offspring will be like this."[42] And when God saw the trusting and unwavering certainty of his spirit, He bare witness unto him by the Holy Spirit, saying in the Scripture: "And Abram

---

40 Genesis 12:1.
41 Genesis 13:15.
42 Genesis 15:5.

trusted God, and it was reckoned to him as righteousness."[43] And he was uncircumcised when this witness was given; and, that the excellency of his faith should be made known by a sign, He gave him circumcision, "a seal of the righteousness of the faith which he had yet being uncircumcised."[44] And after this, according to the promise of God, there was born to him a son, Isaac, from Sarah who was barren. Abraham circumcised him, according to God's covenant. Of Isaac was Jacob born, and in this way the original blessing of Shem reached to Abraham, and from Abraham to Isaac, and from Isaac to Jacob, the inheritance of the Spirit being imparted to them. For the Lord was called the God of Abraham, the God of Isaac, and the God of Jacob. And Jacob had twelve sons, from whom the twelve tribes of Israel were named.

A Nation Is Born

And when a famine had come upon all the earth, it happened that in Egypt alone there was food. So Jacob with all his family moved to Egypt, and the number of them all was seventy-five souls.[45] After four hundred years, as the prophecy had declared beforehand, they had become 660,000. And they were grievously afflicted and oppressed through evil bondage, and sighed and groaned unto the God of their fathers, Abraham and Isaac and Jacob. He brought them out of Egypt by the hand of Moses and Aaron, smiting the Egyptians with ten plagues, and in the last plague sending a destroying angel and slaying their firstborn, both of man and of beast. He saved the children of Israel, revealing in a mystery the sufferings of Christ by the sacrifice of a lamb without spot, and giving its blood to be spread on the doors of the Hebrews for redemption. And the name of this mystery is Passion, the source of deliverance. Dividing the Red Sea, He brought the children of Israel through with all security to the wilderness. The pursuing Egyptians, who followed them and entered

---

43 Genesis 15:6.
44 Romans 4:11.
45 Genesis 46:27 LXX. See also Acts 7:14.

into the sea, were all drowned. This was God's judgment upon those who had sinfully oppressed the descendants of Abraham.

And in the wilderness Moses received the Law from God, "the ten words"[46] on "tablets of stone inscribed by the finger of God."[47] (Now the finger of God is that which is stretched forth from the Father in the Holy Spirit). He delivered the commandments and ordinances to the children of Israel to observe. And he constructed the tabernacle by the command of God, as a visible form of those things which are spiritual and invisible in the heavens, and as a figure of the Church, a prophecy of things to come, in which also were the vessels and the altars of sacrifice and the ark in which he placed the tablets [of the Law]. And he appointed Aaron and his sons as priests, assigning the priesthood to all their tribe, the tribe of Levi. He summoned this whole tribe by the word of God to accomplish the work of service in the temple of God, and gave them the Levitical Law, instructing what sort of men they ought to be who are continually employed in performing the service of the temple of God.

And when they were near to the land which God had promised to Abraham and his descendants, Moses chose a man from every tribe, and sent them to search out the land, its cities, and their inhabitants. At that time God revealed to him the Name which alone is able to save them that believe. So Moses changed the name of Oshea the son of Nun, one of them that were sent, and named him Jesus;[48] and so he sent them with the power of the Name, believing that he should receive them back safe and sound through the guidance of the Name, which came to pass.

Now when they had gone, searched, and enquired, they returned, bringing with them a bunch of grapes. Some of the twelve who were sent cast the whole multitude into fear and dismay, saying that the cities were great and walled, that sons of the giants lived there, and that it was impossible for them to take the land. At this, all the mul-

---

46 Exodus 34:28.
47 Exodus 31:18.
48 Numbers 13:8, 16. "Jesus" and "Joshua" are the same name in Greek, the language in which Irenaeus wrote.

titude wept, failing to believe that God who [had promised to] grant them power and help them overcome. And they also spoke evil of the land, as not being good, and as though it were not worthwhile to undergo the danger for the sake of such a land.

But two of the twelve, Jesus the son of Nun, and Caleb the son of Jephunneh, tore their clothes because of the evil that was done, and begged the people not to be disheartened nor to lose their courage, for God had given all into their hands, and the land was exceeding good. And when the people believed not, but continued in the same unbelief, God changed and altered their way, that they should wander desolate and smitten in the desert. And according to the days that they were in going and returning who had spied out the land—and these were forty in number—setting a year for a day, He kept them in the wilderness for the space of forty years. None of those who were full grown and had understanding counted He worthy to enter into the land because of their unbelief, except the two who had testified of the inheritance, Jesus the son of Nun and Caleb the son of Jephunneh, and those who were quite young and knew not the right hand and the left. So all the unbelieving multitude perished and were consumed in the wilderness, receiving one by one the due reward of their lack of faith. But the children, growing up in the course of forty years, replaced those who died.

THE WORK OF MOSES AND THE PROPHETS

When the forty years were fulfilled, the people drew near to the Jordan, and were assembled over against Jericho. Here Moses gathered the people together, and summarized everything and proclaimed the mighty works of God even unto that day. He prepared those who had grown up in the wilderness to fear God and keep His commandments, imposing on them as it were a new legislation, adding to that which was made before. And this was called Deuteronomy;[49] and in it were written many prophecies concerning our Lord Jesus Christ

---

49 "Deuteronomy" means "second law."

23

and concerning the people, and also concerning the calling of the Gentiles and concerning the kingdom.

And, when Moses had finished his work, God said to him: "Go up into the mountain . . . and you shall die,"[50] for you will not bring in My people into the land. So he "died . . . on account of the word of the Lord."[51] Jesus the son of Nun succeeded him. He divided the Jordan and caused the people to cross over into the land. And when he had overthrown and destroyed the seven races that lived there, he assigned to the people the temporal Jerusalem, where David was king, as was Solomon his son. And Solomon built there a temple to the name of God, according to the likeness of the tabernacle which had been made by Moses after the pattern of the heavenly and spiritual things.

Here the prophets were sent by God through the Holy Spirit, and they instructed the people and turned them to the God of their fathers, the Almighty. The prophets became heralds of the revelation of our Lord Jesus Christ the Son of God, declaring that from the posterity of David His flesh should blossom forth; that after the flesh He would be the son of David, who was the son of Abraham by a long succession. And yet, according to the spirit, He would be the Son of God, pre-existing with the Father, begotten before all the creation of the world; and at the end of time appearing to all the world as man, the Word of God would "gather together" in Himself "all things . . . which are in heaven, and which are on earth."[52]

JESUS IN THE FORM OF MAN

So then He united man with God, and established a community of union between God and man. There was no other way we could partake of incorruption, except by His coming among us. For when incorruption was invisible and unrevealed, it did not help us at all; therefore it became visible, that in all respects we might receive incorruption. And because through Adam all of us were bound with

---

50 Deuteronomy 32:49a, 50a.
51 Deuteronomy 34:5b.
52 Ephesians 1:10.

death through his disobedience, it was right that through the obedience of Him who was made man for us we should be released from death.[53] Because death reigned over the flesh, it was right that through the flesh it should lose its force and let man go free from its oppression. So "the Word was made flesh,"[54] that, through that very flesh which sin had ruled and dominated, it should lose its force and be no longer in us. And therefore our Lord entered into flesh, that He might draw near and contend on behalf of the fathers, and conquer by Adam that which by Adam had stricken us down.

Where did the substance of the first-formed man come from? From the Will and the Wisdom of God, and from the virgin earth. "For God had not sent rain," the Scripture says, "upon the earth," before man was made; "and there was no human to work the earth."[55] From this, then, while it was still virgin, God took dust of the earth and formed the man, the beginning of mankind. So then the Lord, summing up afresh this man Jesus, took the same dispensation of entry into flesh, being born from the Virgin by the Will and the Wisdom of God. This He did that He might show forth the likeness of Adam's entry into flesh, that which was written in the beginning, after the image and likeness of God.[56]

And just as through a disobedient virgin man was stricken down and fell into death, so through the Virgin who was obedient to the Word of God man was recreated and received life. For the Lord came to seek the sheep who were lost, even mankind. For this cause He did not come in some other form, but in that which was descended from Adam He preserved its original likeness. For it was necessary that Adam should be summed up in Christ, that mortality might be conquered by immortality; and Eve summed up in Mary, that a virgin should be a virgin's intercessor, and that a virgin's obedience should undo and put away the disobedience of a virgin.

53 Romans 5:12–21.
54 John 1:14.
55 Genesis 2:5b.
56 See Genesis 1:27.

And the trespass which came by the tree was undone by the tree of obedience, when in obedience to God, the Son of man was nailed to the tree, thereby putting away the knowledge of evil and bringing in and establishing the knowledge of good. Evil is to disobey God, even as hearkening unto God is good. And for this cause the Word spoke by Isaiah the prophet, announcing beforehand that which was to come—for therefore they are prophets, because they proclaim what is to come. By him the Word said, "I do not resist or oppose. I gave my back to the lashes and my cheeks to blows, and I did not turn my face away from the shame of spittings."[57] So then He obeyed "unto death."[58] Hanging on the tree, He put away the old disobedience which was done in the tree. He is the Word of God, who is unseen in our midst but universally present through all the world, and fills its length and breadth and height and depth. For by the Word of God the whole universe is ordered and disposed—in it is crucified the Son of God, inscribed crosswise upon it all. He set upon all things visible the sharing of His cross, that He might show His operation on visible things in a visible form. For He illuminates the height, that is the heavens, and encompasses the deep beneath the earth, and spreads out the length from east to west, and steers across the breadth of north and south, summoning all that are scattered in every quarter to the knowledge of the Father.

Moreover, He fulfilled God's promise to Abraham to make his descendants as the stars of heaven. Christ did this, who was born of a Virgin who was of Abraham's seed, and made those who have faith in Him "lights in the world,"[59] justifying the Gentiles by the same faith as Abraham. For "Abram trusted God, and it was reckoned to him as righteousness."[60] We are also justified by faith in God, for "the righteous one will live by my faith."[61] Now "the promise . . . was not to Abraham . . . through the law, but through . . . faith."[62] Abra-

---

57 Isaiah 50:5b–6.
58 Philippians 2:8.
59 Philippians 2:15b.
60 Genesis 15:6.
61 Habakkuk 2:4.
62 Romans 4:13.

ham was justified by faith, and "the law is not made for a righteous man."[63] In like manner we also are justified, not by the Law, but by faith. This is witnessed to in the Law and in the prophets, whom the Word of God presents to us.

And He fulfilled the promise to David. God had promised him that "from the fruit of your belly" He would raise up an eternal King, whose kingdom should have no end.[64] This King is Christ, the Son of God, who became the Son of man; that is, who became the fruit of a Virgin who was a descendant of David. And for this cause the promise was "from the fruit of your belly," for this expression properly refers to birth from a woman, not "of the fruit of your loins," which would refer to generation from a man. God declared the peculiar uniqueness of the one who was the fruit of the virgin body that was descended from David, the one who was King over the house of David, and whose kingdom will never end.

Thus He gloriously achieved our redemption. He fulfilled the promises to the fathers, and abolished the old disobedience. The Son of God became Son of David and Son of Abraham, perfecting and summing this up in Himself, that He might cause us to possess life. The Word of God was made flesh by means of the Virgin to abolish death and to make man live. For we were imprisoned by sin, being born in sinfulness and living under death.

But God the Father was very merciful. He sent His creative Word,[65] who, coming to deliver us, came to the very place and spot in which we had lost life, and broke our bonds and fetters. His light appeared and made the darkness of the prison disappear, and consecrated our birth and destroyed death. Through the resurrection, He became "the first begotten of the dead."[66] He raised up fallen man, lifting him far above the heaven to the right hand of the glory of the Father, fulfilling God's promise through the prophet, "I will raise up the tent of

---

63   1 Timothy 1:9.
64   Psalm 132 (131 LXX):11b.
65   Irenaeus calls Jesus God's "creative Word," calling to mind John 1:3, which says that all things
      were created by God's Word or *Logos*. See also Colossians 1:16.
66   Revelation 1:5.

David that has fallen,"[67] that is, the flesh that was from David. Our Lord Jesus Christ truly fulfilled this when He gloriously achieved our redemption. He truly raises us up, making us free unto the Father. And if any man will not believe in His birth from a Virgin, how shall he believe in His resurrection from the dead? It would not be wonderful or astonishing or extraordinary if someone who was not even born rose from the dead. We cannot even speak of a resurrection of someone who came into being without being born. For one who is unborn and immortal will not experience death. For if one took not the beginning of man, how could he receive man's end?

If He was not born, neither did He die. If He did not die, neither did He rise from the dead. If He rose not from the dead, neither did He vanquish death and bring its reign to nothing. If death is not vanquished, how can we ascend to life, who from the beginning have fallen under death? Therefore those who take away redemption from man and do not believe that God will raise them from the dead also despise the birth of our Lord. He was born on our behalf, so that the Word of God should be made flesh in order to manifest the resurrection of the flesh, and that He might have preeminence over all things in the heavens, as the first-born and eldest offspring of the thought of the Father, as the Word, fulfilling all things and guiding and ruling upon earth. For He was the Virgin's firstborn, a just and holy man, God-fearing, good, well-pleasing to God, perfect in all ways, and delivering from hell all who follow Him. He was "the first begotten of the dead,"[68] the Prince and Author of life unto God.

THE PREEMINENCE OF THE WORD

Thus the Word of God has the preeminence in all things.[69] He is true man and "Wonderful, Counsellor, The mighty God."[70] He calls

---

67   Amos 9:11; Acts 15:16.
68   Revelation 1:5.
69   Colossians 1:18.
70   Isaiah 9:6 KJV (9:5 LXX). Irenaeus here quotes from the version of this verse reflecting the Hebrew Masoretic Text and some Septuagint variants. He later quotes the verse as included in other Septuagint manuscripts, which calls the promised Child the "Messenger of the Great Council" and does not include "mighty God." Irenaeus was familiar with both variants since he quoted both.

men anew to fellowship with God, and by fellowship with Him we partake of incorruption. He was proclaimed by the Law through Moses, and by the prophets of the Most High and Almighty God, as Son of the Father of all, and as He by whom all things exist. He who in old time spoke with Moses came into Judaea, generated from God by the Holy Spirit, and was born of the Virgin Mary, even of her who was of the seed of David and of Abraham. In this way, Jesus, the Anointed of God, showed Himself to be the One who was proclaimed beforehand by the prophets.

His forerunner was John the Baptist, who prepared the people to receive the Word of life. John declared that Jesus was the Christ, on whom the Spirit of God rested, mingling with His flesh. Jesus' disciples—who witnessed all His good deeds, His teachings, His sufferings, His death, His resurrection, and His ascension into heaven—became apostles. After receiving the power of the Holy Spirit, they were sent out by Him into all the world, and accomplished the calling of the Gentiles, showing to mankind the way of life. They turned the Gentiles from idols, fornication, and covetousness, cleansing their souls and bodies by the baptism of water and of the Holy Spirit. This Holy Spirit they had received from the Lord, and they distributed and imparted It to those who believed. Thus they ordered and established the churches. By faith, love, and hope, they established that which was foretold by the prophets, even the calling of the Gentiles, according to the mercy of God which was extended to them. Through their ministries, they revealed this calling of the Gentiles, admitting them into the promise of the fathers. Those who believed in and loved the Lord, and continued in holiness and righteousness and patient endurance, were promised eternal life from God by the resurrection of the dead, through Jesus Christ, who died and rose again, to whom God has given the kingdom of all existing things, authority over the living and the dead, and also the judgment. The apostles taught the Gentiles by the Word of truth to keep their flesh undefiled and their soul unstained for the resurrection.

This is how those who believe live, since the Holy Spirit continually abides in them. The Holy Spirit was given by Christ in baptism, and is retained by the receiver if he walks in truth, holiness, righteousness, and patient endurance. This Spirit will give resurrection to those who believe, the body receiving the soul again, and along with it, by the power of the Holy Spirit, is raised up and enters into the kingdom of God. This is the fruit of the blessing of Japheth, in the calling of the Gentiles, made manifest through the Church, ready to receive its dwelling in the house of Shem according to the promise of God. The Spirit of God declared beforehand by the prophets that all these things would happen, so that the faith of those who worship God in truth should be confirmed. God made known beforehand through the prophets that events would occur which would be impossible to human nature, and these prophecies would cause men to be incredulous. Then, when these incredible things at last came to pass, as they had been foretold long before, we would know it was God who thus proclaimed to us beforehand our redemption.

So then we must believe all that God says, for in all things God is true. Now that there was a Son of God, and that this Son existed not only before He appeared in the world, but also before the world was made, Moses (who was the first who prophesied) testifies in Hebrew: "*Baresith bara Elowin basan benuam samenthares.*" And this, being translated into our language, is: "The Son in the beginning God established then the heaven and the earth."[71] Jeremiah the prophet also testified: "Before the morning, I fathered you; before the sun his name will remain."[72] So the Son existed before the creation of the world and the stars. Again, he says: "Blessed is he who was, before he became man."[73] For God the Son was at the beginning, before the creation of the world. But for us, it seemed that He began when He appeared as a human. Before that, we did not

---

71 This reading of Genesis 1:1 is found nowhere but in this work.
72 Psalm 110 (109 LXX):3b; Psalm 72 (71 LXX):17b. Irenaeus mistakenly attributes this quotation to Jeremiah although it is a composite of two verses from Psalms.
73 The original source of this quotation is unknown. Lactantius (c. 250–c. 325) quotes the same saying (*Divine Institutes* 4.8) and also attributes it to Jeremiah. The heterodox gospels of Thomas (Saying 19) and Philip (64:10) both attribute similar sayings to Jesus.

know Him, and He "was not" to us. Wherefore His disciple John, in teaching us who the Son of God is, says: "In the beginning was the Word, and the Word was with God, and the Word was God. The same was in the beginning with God. All things were made by him; and without him was not any thing made that was made."[74] Here John shows with certainty that the Word, who was in the beginning with the Father, and by whom all things were made, is God's Son.

THE WORD SPEAKS TO MEN
Moses tells how the Son of God talked with Abraham.

> God appeared to him near the oak of Mamre while he was sitting at the door of his tent during midday. Upon looking up, he saw with his eyes, and look, three men had stood over him, and upon seeing them, he ran up from the doorway of his tent to meet them and he bowed down to the earth, and he said, "Lord, if perhaps I have found favor before you."[75]

In the rest of the passage, he spoke with the Lord, and the Lord spoke with him. Now two of the three were angels, but one was the Son of God, with whom also Abraham spoke, pleading on behalf of the men of Sodom, that they should not perish if at least ten righteous would be found there. While Abraham and the Son of God were speaking, the two angels entered into Sodom, and Lot received them. And then the Scripture says: "And the Lord rained sulfur and fire on Sodom and Gomorrah from the Lord out of the heavens."[76] The Son, who spoke with Abraham, being "Lord," received power to punish the men of Sodom "from the Lord out of the heavens," even from the Father who rules over all. So Abraham was a prophet, for he saw things to come. He saw that the Son of God would someday come in human form and speak with men and eat with them, and then should bring in the judgment from the Father, having received from Him who rules over all the power to punish the men of Sodom.

---

74 John 1:1–3.
75 Genesis 18:1–3a.
76 Genesis 19:24.

Jacob, when he went into Mesopotamia, saw Him in a dream, standing upon the ladder,[77] that is, the tree [cross], which was set up from earth to heaven. For by the cross those who believe on Him go up to the heavens. His sufferings are our ascension on high. All such visions point to the Son of God, speaking with men and being in their midst. The Father and Maker of all, who is not seen by the world, said, "Heaven is my throne, and the earth is a footstool for my feet; what sort of house will you build for me? And what sort of place will you build as my place of repose?"[78] He measures "the heaven in his span and the whole earth with his measure."[79] It was not this Father who came and stood in a very small space and spoke with Abraham. It was the Word of God, who was ever with mankind, made known beforehand what would happen in the future, and taught men the things of God.

He spoke with Moses in the bush, and said, "Having observed, I know the suffering distress of my people that is in Egypt . . . and I have come down to rescue them."[80] He came down for the deliverance of the oppressed, bringing us out from the power of the Egyptians, that is, from all idolatry and impiety. He delivered us from the Red Sea, that is, saved us from the deadly confusion of the Gentiles and their grievous blasphemy. The Word of God prepared and rehearsed beforehand the things concerning us. In those times, He set forth in types the things which were to be. Now in reality He has brought us out from the cruel service of the Gentiles, and a stream of water in the desert He has made to flow from a rock. That Rock is Himself, and He has given twelve fountains, that is, the teaching of the twelve apostles. The obstinate unbelievers He has brought to an end and consumed in the wilderness, but those who believed on Him, and in malice were children,[81] He made to enter into the inheritance of the fathers. We receive possession of the heritage, not by Moses, but by

---

77 Genesis 28:12–13.
78 Isaiah 66:1. See also Acts 7:49.
79 Isaiah 40:12.
80 Exodus 3:7–8.
81 1 Corinthians 14:20.

Jesus,[82] who also delivers us from Amalek by the spreading of His hands,[83] and brings us to the kingdom of the Father.

So then the Father is Lord and the Son is Lord, and the Father is God and the Son is God, for that which is begotten of God is God. In the substance and power of His being, there is shown forth one God, but there is also, according to the plan of our redemption, both Son and Father. To created things the Father of all is invisible and unapproachable; therefore those who are to draw near to God must access the Father through the Son. David speaks even more clearly concerning the Father and the Son as follows: "Your throne, O God, is for eternity of eternity. . . . You loved righteousness and hated lawlessness. On account of this, God . . . anointed you with olive oil of great joy beyond your companions."[84] For the Son, as God, receives from the Father, that is, from God, the throne of the everlasting kingdom, and the oil of anointing above His fellows. The oil of anointing is the Spirit, with which He has been anointed. His fellows are the prophets, righteous men and apostles, and all His disciples, who receive the fellowship of His kingdom.

THE PRE-EXISTENCE OF THE SON WITH THE FATHER
David says further:

> The Lord said to my Lord, "Be seated at my right side until I set your enemies as a footstool for your feet." The Lord will send out a rod of power from Zion, "Rule in the middle of your enemies. With you is authority in the day of your power, with the splendor of the holy ones. From the womb, before the morning, I fathered you." The Lord swore and will not regret, "You are a priest for eternity according to the order of Melchizedek." The Lord at your right hand crushed together kings in the day of his anger. He will judge among the nations. He will fill up with corpses. He will crush the heads of many upon the earth. From a torrent in the way he will drink. On account of this he will raise up his head.[85]

---

82 "Jesus" and "Joshua" are the same in Greek.
83 The early Christians saw the extension of Moses' arms on this occasion as a type of the cross of Christ.
84 Psalm 45 (44 LXX):7–8. See also Hebrews 1:8–9.
85 Psalm 110 (109 LXX).

Now by this he proclaimed that He came into being before all things, and that He rules over and judges all mankind, even kings who hate Him and persecute His name; for these are His enemies. In calling Him God's priest forever, he declared His immortality. And therefore he said: "From a torrent in the way he will drink. On account of this he will raise up his head,"[86] proclaiming the exaltation with glory that followed His humanity, humiliation, and ingloriousness.

Isaiah the prophet says: "This is what the Lord God says to my anointed[87] Lord, whose right hand I have grasped so that nations obey before him."[88] And how the Christ is called Son of God and King of the Gentiles, that is, of all mankind, and that He is not only called, but is in fact, the Son of God and King of all, David declares thus: "The Lord said to me, 'You are my son; today I have fathered you. Ask from me, and I will give to you the nations as your inheritance, and as your possession the ends of the earth.'"[89] These things were not said of David, for he did not reign over the Gentiles nor the ends of the earth, but only over the Jews. Therefore it is plain that the promise to the Anointed to reign over the ends of the earth is to the Son of God, whom David himself acknowledges as his Lord, saying thus: "The Lord said to my Lord, 'Be seated at my right side.'"[90] He means that the Father speaks with the Son, as we showed a little before through Isaiah, who said: "The Lord God says to my anointed Lord . . . that nations obey before him."[91] For the same promise is made by the two prophets, that He would be King, so that the speech of God is addressed to one and the same, namely to Christ the Son of God. And as David says: "The Lord said to me,"[92] it is necessary to say that it is not David who speaks, nor any one of the prophets,

---

86 Psalm 110 (109 LXX):7.
87 "Christ" (*Christos*) in Greek, and "Messiah" (*Meshiach*) in Hebrew, mean "Anointed."
88 Isaiah 45:1. Modified from the Lexham English Septuagint. Irenaeus' copy of the Septuagint apparently read "to my anointed Lord (*kurio*)" instead of "to my anointed Cyrus (*Kuro*)." This alternate reading is quoted in other early Christian writings as well.
89 Psalm 2:7–8.
90 Psalm 110 (109 LXX):1.
91 Isaiah 45:1. Modified from the Lexham English Septuagint.
92 Psalm 110 (109 LXX):1.

in his own person. For it is not a man who speaks the prophecies; but the Spirit of God, assimilating and likening Himself to the persons represented, speaks in the prophets and utters the words, sometimes from Christ and sometimes from the Father.

So then it is fitting that Christ says through David that He converses with the Father, and He rightly says the other things concerning Himself through the prophets. Here is another example from Isaiah:

> And now this is what the Lord—who formed me from the belly as his bondservant in order to gather Jacob and Israel to himself—says: "I will be gathered and glorified before the Lord, and God will be strength for me." And he said to me, "It is a great thing for you to be called my servant,[93] to establish the tribes of Jacob and to return the dispersion of Israel. Look! I have given you as a covenant for a nation, as a light for the nations so that you may become salvation as far as the end of the earth."[94]

Here, first of all, it is seen that the Son of God pre-existed, that the Father spoke with Him and revealed Him to men before He was born. Next, He must be born a man among men, and that the same God "formed" Him "from the belly," that is, that He should be born of the Spirit of God. Also, He is the Lord of all men and the Savior of those who believe on Him, both Jews and others. For the Jews are called "Israel" in the Hebrew language, from Jacob their father, who was the first to be called Israel, and He calls the whole of mankind "Gentiles." The Son of the Father calls Himself "servant" because of His subjection to the Father, for among men every son is the servant of his father.

Christ, then, being the Son of God before all the world, is with the Father, and being with the Father is also near and close and joined unto mankind. He is King of all, because the Father has subjected all things unto Him. He is the Savior of those who believe on Him. The [prophetic] Scriptures declare such things. It is not feasible to enu-

---

93 The Greek word *paida* used by the Septuagint translator of Isaiah can mean either "child" (specifically a boy), as rendered by the Lexham English Septuagint in this verse, or "servant." Irenaeus understood it to mean "servant" here, as his following commentary makes clear.

94 Isaiah 49:5–6. Modified from the Lexham English Septuagint.

merate every Scripture in order, but from these examples you may understand other similar prophecies. To understand what has been spoken by the prophets, believe in Christ and seek understanding and comprehension from God.

THE VIRGIN BIRTH

Now that this Christ, who was with the Father, being the Word of the Father, was to become man and undergo the process of birth, be born of a virgin, and dwell among men, the Father of all bringing about His incarnation, Isaiah says:

> "Because of this, the Lord himself will give you a sign: Look, the virgin will conceive in the womb and will bear a son, and you will call his name Immanuel. He will eat butter and honey before he knows either to prefer evil or choose the good." Because before the child knows good or bad, he resists wickedness to choose good.[95]

So he proclaimed the virgin birth. And that He was truly man he declared beforehand by His eating, and also because he called Him "the child," and further by giving Him a name, for this is the custom also for one who is born. And His name is two-fold: in the Hebrew tongue "Messiah Jesus," and in ours "Christ Savior."[96] The two names are names of works actually accomplished. He was named Christ [Anointed] because through Him the Father anointed and adorned all things. On His coming as man, He was anointed with the Spirit of God and His Father. Through Isaiah, He says of Himself: "The Spirit of the Lord is upon me, on account of which he has anointed me; he has sent me to bring good news to the poor."[97] He was named Savior because He became the cause of salvation to those who at that time were delivered by Him from all sicknesses and from death, and to those who afterwards believed on Him, the author of salvation, in the future and for evermore. For this cause, then, He is the Savior.

---

95   Isaiah 7:14–16a.
96   "Messiah" and "Christ" are equivalent in Hebrew and Greek, respectively. "Jesus" means "Jehovah Saves."
97   Isaiah 61:1. Jesus applied this prophecy to Himself in Luke 4:18, 21.

Now Emmanuel is, being interpreted, "With you God;" or as a yearning cry uttered by the prophet, such as this: "With us shall be God;" according to which it is the explanation and manifestation of the good tidings proclaimed. For, "Look," He says, "Look, the virgin will conceive in the womb and will bear a son,"[98] and He, being God, is to be with us. And, as if altogether astonished at these things, he proclaims in regard to these future events that "with us shall be God." And yet again concerning His birth, the same prophet says in another place, "Before the one in labor gave birth, before the distress of birth pangs arrived, she escaped and bore a male child."[99] Thus he showed that His birth from the Virgin was unforeseen and unexpected. And again the same prophet says: "For unto us a child is born, unto us a son is given ... and his name shall be called Wonderful, Counsellor, The mighty God."[100]

He calls Him "Wonderful Counsellor," meaning [He is counsellor] of the Father. Thus it is declared that the Father works all things together with Him, as is contained in the first book of Moses which is called Genesis: "And God said, 'Let us make humankind according to our image and according to our likeness.'"[101] Here the Father is speaking to the Son, the Wonderful Counsellor of the Father. Moreover, He is also our Counsellor, giving advice; not compelling us as God, even though He is "mighty God," as he says, but giving advice that we should forsake ignorance and acquire knowledge, depart from error and come to the truth, and put away corruption and receive incorruption.

Again Isaiah says:

> And they will be willing, if they became burnt. Because a child was born to us; a son was given to us whose leadership came upon his shoulder; and his name is called "Messenger of the Great Council,"[102] for I will bring peace upon the rulers and health to him. His leadership is great, and there is no

---

98 Isaiah 7:14.
99 Isaiah 66:7.
100 Isaiah 9:6. In this instance, Irenaeus' quotation reflects the Masoretic and some Septuagint manuscripts which include "mighty God."
101 Genesis 1:26a.
102 Here Irenaeus again quotes the Septuagint version without "mighty God."

> boundary to his peace on the throne of David and his kingdom, to establish and take hold of it by justice and by righteousness, from now to eternity.[103]

The Son of God is proclaimed both as being born, and also as eternal King. "They will be willing, if they became burnt" is said of those who do not believe on Him, and who have done to Him all that they have done. They shall say in the judgment, "How much better that we had been burned with fire before the Son of God was born, than that, when He was born, we should not have believed on Him." Because for those who died before Christ appeared, there is hope that in the judgment of the risen they may obtain salvation, even those who feared God, died in righteousness, and had in them the Spirit of God, such as the patriarchs, prophets, and righteous men. But for those who, after Christ's appearing, did not believe on Him, there is a vengeance without pardon in the judgment. Now in this: "whose leadership came upon his shoulder," the cross on which He was nailed is declared symbolically. For that which was and is a reproach to Him, and for His sake to us, even the cross, this same, says he, is His "leadership," a sign of His kingdom. "Messenger of the Great Council"—that is, of the Father whom He has declared unto us.

THE SON OF DAVID

From what has been said, it is plain how the prophets revealed beforehand that the Son of God would be born, in what way He was to be born, and that He would be shown to be the Christ. They also proclaimed beforehand in what land and among what people He was to be born and appear. Moses says in Genesis:

> A ruler will not cease from Judah, and one who leads from his thighs, until he comes for whom it is reserved,[104] and he is the expectation of nations . . . he will wash his garment in wine and his cloak in the blood of grapes.[105]

---

103 Isaiah 9:5b–7a.
104 The Lexham English Septuagint here reads "until the things laid away for him come." Irenaeus here uses a variant reading also quoted by Justin Martyr (*First Apology* 32:1; *Dialogue* 120).
105 Genesis 49:10–11. Modified from the Lexham English Septuagint.

Now Judah, the son of Jacob, was the ancestor of the Jews; through him they obtained the name. There failed not a prince among them and a leader, until the coming of Christ. But from the time of His coming the might of the quiver was captured, the land of the Jews was given over into subjection to the Romans, and they had no longer a prince or king of their own. For He was come, "for whom . . . is reserved" in heaven the kingdom, who also "washed his garment in wine and his cloak in the blood of grapes." His robe and His garment are those who believe on Him, whom He cleansed, redeeming us by His blood. And His blood is said to be "blood of the grape." For just as no man makes the blood of the grape, but God produces it, and it "delights" those who drink it,[106] so also His flesh and blood no man produced, but God made. The Lord Himself gave the sign of the Virgin, even that Emmanuel which was from the Virgin,[107] who also "delights" those who drink of Him, that is to say, who receive His Spirit, everlasting gladness. He is the "expectation of nations," of those who hope in Him, because we expect that He will reestablish the kingdom.

Moses[108] says: "A star will rise up out of Jacob, and a leader[109] will be established out of Israel."[110] This shows even more clearly that He would come in the flesh from among the Jews. From Jacob and from the tribe of Judah He was born. He came down from heaven, and fulfilled this prophecy when the "star" appeared in heaven. By "leader" he means king, because He is the King of all the redeemed. At His birth the star appeared to the Magi who dwelt in the east, and thereby they learned that Christ was born. They came to Judaea, led by the star, until the star came to Bethlehem where Christ was born. They entered the house where the child was lying, wrapped in swaddling clothes, and [the star] stood over His head, declaring to the Magi the Son of God, the Christ.

---

106 Psalm 104 (103 LXX):15.
107 Isaiah 7:14.
108 Balaam, as recorded by Moses.
109 Irenaeus' version reads "leader" where the LXX has "man" ("person" in the Lexham English Septuagint). The Masoretic Text reads "Scepter."
110 Numbers 24:17b. Modified from the Lexham English Septuagint.

Moreover, Isaiah himself says:

> And a rod will emerge from the root of Jesse, and a flower will come up from the root. And God's spirit will rest on him, a spirit of wisdom and intelligence, a spirit of counsel and strength, a spirit of knowledge and piety. He will fill him with a spirit of the fear of God; he will not judge according to reputation or reprove according to speech. Rather, he will render fair judgment to a low one, and he will have compassion on[111] the low of the land; and he will strike the land with the word of his mouth, and with breath through his lips he will destroy ungodly things. And he will be girded at the waist with righteousness and enclosed with truth at his sides. And a wolf will feed together with a lamb, and a leopard will rest with a kid, and a little calf and a bull and a lion will feed together. . . . And an infant child will lay its hand on an asp's hole and on a bed of asps' offspring. And they shall surely do no wrong. . . . And in that day there will be the root of Jesse and the one who rises up to rule nations; nations will put their hope in him, and his rising[112] will be honor.[113]

By these words he states that He was born from her who was of the race of David and of Abraham. For Jesse was the descendant of Abraham, and the father of David, and David's descendant was the virgin who conceived Christ. Now as to the "rod," for this cause also Moses showed mighty works to Pharaoh with a rod. With other men also, the rod is a sign of rule. By "flower" he means His flesh, for from the Spirit it budded forth, as we have said before.

"He will not judge according to reputation or reprove according to speech. Rather, he will render fair judgment to a low one, and he will have compassion on the low of the land."[114] By this he clearly establishes and declares His divinity. To judge without respect of persons and partiality, to not favor the illustrious, but afford worthy and equal treatment to the humble, accords with the height and summit of the righteousness of God. God is influenced and moved by none except the righteous. To show mercy is the peculiar attribute of God, who is able to save by His mercy. "He will strike the land with the word of his mouth," "destroy ungodly things" with only a

---

111 The Septuagint here reads "reprove."
112 The Septuagint here reads "rest." This reading is unique to Irenaeus.
113 Isaiah 11:1–6, 8–9a, 10. Modified from the Lexham English Septuagint.
114 Isaiah 11:3b–4a. Modified from the Lexham English Septuagint.

word[115]—this power belongs to God, who works all things with a word. And in saying "he will be girded at the waist with righteousness and enclosed with truth at his sides,"[116] he declares His human form and aspect, and His own surpassing righteousness.

Now as to the union and peace of the animals of different kinds, which by nature are opposed and hostile to each other, the Elders say[117] that this will happen literally at the coming of Christ, when He is to reign over all. For already in a symbol he announces the gathering together in peace and concord, through the name of Christ, of men of different races but similar dispositions. When thus united, the righteous, who are likened to calves, lambs, kids, and nursing children, receive no hurt at all from those who formerly, through their greed, were like wild beasts in manners and disposition, both men and women. Some of them were like wolves and lions, ravaging the weaker and warring on their equals, while the women were like leopards or asps, who slew, it may be, even their loved ones with deadly poisons, or by reason of lustful desire. But now, coming together in one name, they have acquired righteous habits by the grace of God, changing their wild and untamed nature. This has happened already. Those who previously were exceedingly wicked, so that they left no work of ungodliness undone, learning of Christ and believing on Him, have at once believed and been changed, so as to leave no excellency of righteousness undone. So great is the transformation which faith in Christ, the Son of God, accomplishes for those who believe on Him! And he says: "One who rises up to rule nations," because He is to die and rise again, and be confessed and believed in as the Son of God and King. On this account he says: "And his rising shall be honor," that is, glory; for when He rose, then He was glorified as divine.

---

115 Isaiah 11:4b.

116 Isaiah 11:5.

117 "The Elders" probably refers to those church leaders who had personally known the apostles. In his *Against Heresies*, Irenaeus refers several times to a person he calls "the Elder," but he does not give this elder's name. Who he was is unknown and controversial. It has been suggested that he was Polycarp, but Irenaeus did mention Polycarp by name in *Against Heresies*, so it would seem strange for him to refer to Polycarp in this cryptic fashion elsewhere in the same work.

Again the prophet says: "On that day I will raise up the tent of David that has fallen;"[118] that is, the body of Christ, which, as we have said before, was born of David, which he plainly declares as rising from the dead after death. For the body is called a tabernacle. By these words he says that He who according to the flesh is of the race of David will be Christ the Son of God, that He will die and rise again, and that He is in aspect a man, but in power God, and that He Himself will be judge of all the world, the only worker of righteousness and redeemer. All this the [prophetic] Scripture declared.

The prophet Micah speaks of the place where Christ should be born, that it should be in Bethlehem of Judaea, saying: "And you, O Bethlehem, house of Ephrathah, you are very small to be in the thousands of Judah, from which for me one will come out to be for a ruler of Israel."[119] Bethlehem is the native place of David, so that not only in respect of the Virgin who bore Him is He of David's race, but also because of His birth in Bethlehem, the native place of David.

David says that of his race Christ is to be born, speaking after this manner:

> Because of David, your servant, do not turn back the face of your anointed one.[120] The Lord swore to David truthfulness, and he will never reject it, "From the fruit of your belly I will establish upon your throne; if your sons will keep my covenant and my testimonies, these things that I will teach them, and their sons will sit upon your throne until eternity."[121]

But none of the sons of David reigned forever, nor was their kingdom forever, for it was brought to nothing. But the king that was born of David, He is Christ. All these testimonies declare in plain terms His descent according to the flesh, and the race and place where He was to be born, so that no man should seek among the Gentiles or elsewhere for the birth of the Son of God, but in Bethlehem of Judaea, from Abraham and David's race.

---

118 Amos 9:11; Acts 15:16.
119 Micah 5:2; Matthew 2:6.
120 "Anointed one" is *Christos* (Christ) in Greek.
121 Psalm 132 (131 LXX):10–12.

TRIUMPHAL ENTRY

About the manner of His entry into Jerusalem, which was the capital of Judaea, the prophet Isaiah declares: "Tell ye the daughter of Sion, Behold, thy King cometh unto thee, meek, and sitting upon an ass, and a colt the foal of an ass."[122] For, sitting on an ass's colt, He entered into Jerusalem, the multitudes laying down their garments for Him. And by "the daughter of Sion" he means Jerusalem.

So then, the prophets declared that the Son of God would be born, in what manner He would be born, where He was to be born, and that Christ is the one eternal King. They also foretold how He, sprung from mankind, should heal those whom He healed, raise the dead whom He raised, and be hated, despised, suffer, and be put to death and crucified, even as Jesus was hated, despised, and put to death.

HEALINGS

At this point, let us speak of His healings. Isaiah says thus: "Himself took our infirmities, and bare our sicknesses,"[123] that is to say, He shall take, and shall bear. For there are passages in which the Spirit of God through the prophets states future things in past tense. That which God has determined will take place, is reckoned as having already taken place, and the Spirit, seeing the time when the prophecy is fulfilled, utters the words accordingly. Concerning the kind of healing, thus will He make mention, saying: "And on that day deaf people will hear the words of a scroll, and the eyes of blind people will see in the darkness and in the fog."[124] And He says again: "Be strong, hands at ease and feeble knees! Give comfort, fainthearted in mind! Be strong; do not be frightened! Look, our God is repaying judgment, and he will repay! He himself will come and save us! Then blind people's eyes will be opened, and dumb people's ears will hear. Then the lame will leap like a deer, and the stammerer's tongue will

---

122 Matthew 21:5, quoting from Zechariah 9:9; cf. Isaiah 62:11.
123 Matthew 8:17b; Isaiah 53:4a.
124 Isaiah 29:18.

be clear."[125] Concerning the dead, He says: "The dead will rise, and those in the tombs will be raised."[126] In bringing these things to pass, He shall be believed to be the Son of God.

THE MESSIAH'S SUFFERINGS AND CRUCIFIXION

And that He would be despised, tormented, and in the end put to death, Isaiah says:

> Look! My child will understand and be raised up and be magnified very much. The way many will be impressed by you, so your appearance will be despised by people and your glory by the people, Thus many nations will be impressed at him, and kings will shut their mouth, because those to whom it has not been declared concerning him will see, and those who have not heard will understand. O Lord, who has believed our report? And to whom has the arm of the Lord been revealed? We proclaimed as a child before him, as a root in a thirsty land. He has no appearance or glory. And we saw him, and he had no appearance or beauty. Instead, his appearance was dishonored and coming to an end among the sons of humans, a human who is in misfortune and who knows how to bear sickness, for his face has been turned back; he was dishonored and was not esteemed. This one carries our sins and suffers pain for us, and we regarded him as one who is in difficulty, misfortune, and affliction. But he was wounded because of our sins, and he became weakened because of our lawless acts. The discipline of our peace was upon him; by his bruise we were healed.[127]

By these words it is declared that He was tormented. David also says: "And I was flogged."[128] Now David was never flogged, but Christ was, when the command was given that He should be crucified. Isaiah, by His Word, says: "I gave my back to the lashes and my cheeks to blows, and I did not turn my face away from the shame of spittings."[129] And Jeremiah the prophet says the same: "He will give his cheek to the one who strikes him; he will be fed with reproaches."[130] All these things Christ suffered.

---

125 Isaiah 35:3–6a.
126 Isaiah 26:19a.
127 Isaiah 52:13–53:5.
128 Psalm 73 (72 LXX):14.
129 Isaiah 50:6.
130 Lamentations 3:30.

Now what follows in Isaiah is this: "By his bruise we were healed. We all have been misled like sheep; each person was misled in his own path, and the Lord handed him over for our sins."[131] It is manifest therefore that by the will of the Father these things occurred to Him for the sake of our salvation. Then he says: "And because he was afflicted, he does not open his mouth; like a sheep is led to slaughter, and like a lamb is voiceless before the one who shears it, so he does not open his mouth."[132] Behold how he declares His voluntary coming to death. And when the prophet says: "His judgment was taken away in humiliation,"[133] he signifies the appearance of His humiliation; according to the form of the abasement was the taking away of judgment. This taking away of judgment is for some unto salvation, and to some unto the torments of perdition. For there is a taking away *for* a person, and also *from* a person. So also with the judgment—those *for* whom it is taken away have it unto the torments of their perdition, but those *from* whom it is taken away are saved by it. Now those who crucified Him took away to themselves the judgment, and when they had done this to Him, they did not believe on Him. Through that judgment which was taken away by them, they shall be destroyed with torments. From them who believe on Him the judgment is taken away, and they are no longer under it. The judgment is the fiery destruction of the unbelievers at the end of the world.

Then he says: "Who will describe his generation?"[134] This was said to warn us, lest through His enemies and the outrage of His sufferings we should despise Him as a lowly and contemptible man. For He who endured all this has an undeclarable generation, that is, His [genealogical] descent. He who is His Father is undeclarable and unspeakable. Know therefore that such descent was His who endured these sufferings. Despise Him not because of the sufferings,

---

131 Isaiah 53:5b–6.
132 Isaiah 53:7.
133 Isaiah 53:8a.
134 Isaiah 53:8b NETS LXX.

which for your sake He purposefully endured, but fear Him because of His descent.

In another place Jeremiah says: "The spirit [breath][135] of our face, the Lord Christ [anointed Lord], was captured by their destructions, of whom we said, 'We will live in its shade among the nations.'"[136] This Scripture declares that Christ, being the Spirit of God, was to become a suffering man, and [the prophetic writer] is, as it were, amazed and astonished at His sufferings, that in such manner He was to endure sufferings, "of whom we said, 'We will live in its shade.'" By "shade" he means His body. Just as a shadow is made by a body, so also Christ's body was made by His Spirit. The "shade" also indicates the humiliation and contemptibility of His body, for as the shadow of bodies standing upright is upon the ground and is trodden upon, so also the body of Christ fell upon the ground by His sufferings and was trodden on indeed. He also called Christ's body a shadow because the Spirit overshadowed it and covered it with glory. Moreover, often when the Lord passed by, they laid those who were suffering from diseases in the way, and whoever His shadow fell on was healed.[137]

And again the same prophet says concerning the sufferings of Christ:

> Look how the righteous has perished and no one takes it to heart, and righteous men are taken away and no one comprehends. For the righteous has been taken away from the face of injustice; his burial will be in peace; he will be taken up out of the middle.[138]

Who else is perfectly righteous, but the Son of God, who makes righteous and perfects those who believe on Him, who like Him are persecuted and put to death? But in saying "his burial will be in peace," he declares how on account of our redemption He died, for it is in the peace of redemption. This also shows that by His death

---

135 In both Greek and Hebrew, "spirit" and "breath" are the same word.
136 Lamentations 4:20. Modified from the Lexham English Septuagint.
137 cf. Acts 5:15.
138 Isaiah 57:1–2.

those who were previously enemies and opposed to one another, believing with one accord upon Him, should have peace with one another, becoming friends and beloved on account of their common faith in Him, which has now happened. But in saying "he will be taken up out of the middle," he signifies His resurrection from the dead. Moreover, because He appeared no more after His death and burial, the prophet declares that after dying and rising again He was to remain immortal, saying: "He asked you for life, and you gave him length of days for eternity of eternity."[139] Now what is this that he says, "He asked you for life," since He was about to die? He proclaims His resurrection from the dead, and that, being raised from the dead, He is immortal. For He received both "life," that He should rise, and "length of days for eternity of eternity," that He should be incorruptible.

And again David says this concerning the death and resurrection of Christ: "I went to bed and fell asleep. I awoke, because the Lord will help me."[140] David did not say this about himself, for he was not raised after death, but the Spirit of Christ, who spoke also in other prophets concerning Him, says here by David, "I went to bed and fell asleep. I awoke, because the Lord will help me." By "asleep" He means death, for He arose again.

Again David says concerning the sufferings of Christ: "Why were the nations unruly, and the people meditated on vain things? The kings of the earth are present, and the rulers are gathered together against the Lord and against his anointed one."[141] For Herod, the king of the Jews, and Pontius Pilate, the governor of Claudius Caesar,[142] came together and condemned Him to be crucified. Herod was afraid that he would be expelled from his kingdom by Christ, as though He were to be an earthly king. Pilate was constrained against his will by Herod and the Jews who were with him to deliver Him

---

139 Psalm 21:4 (20:5 LXX).
140 Psalm 3:5 (3:6 LXX).
141 Psalm 2:1–2.
142 Pilate (r. AD 27–37) was actually Procurator of Judaea under the Emperor Tiberius.

to death, [for they threatened him] that to release a man who was called a king would be to act contrary to Caesar.

The same prophet says further about the sufferings of Christ:

> But you rejected and scorned. You postponed your anointed one. You overturned the covenant of your servant. You profaned to the earth his sanctuary. You destroyed all his fences. You placed his strongholds as cowardice. All those who traveled through the road plundered him. He became a reproach to his neighbors. You lifted high the right hand of his enemies. You made all his enemies cheerful. You turned away the help of his sword, and you did not help him in the battle. You deprived him from purification. You broke down his throne to the earth. You diminished the days of his throne. You poured shame over him. [143]

He clearly declared that He should endure these things by the will of the Father, for by the will of the Father He was to endure sufferings.

And Zechariah says this: "A sword has been raised up against my shepherds and against my male citizen,' says the Lord Almighty.[144] 'I will smite the shepherd, and the sheep of the flock shall be scattered abroad.'"[145] And this came to pass when He was taken by the Jews. All the disciples forsook Him, fearing lest they should die with Him. For they did not yet steadfastly believe on Him, until they had seen Him risen from the dead.

Again He says in the Twelve Prophets,[146] "And they bound him and brought him as a present to the king."[147] Pontius Pilate was governor of Judaea, and he had at that time resentful enmity against Herod the king of the Jews. But then, when Christ was brought to him bound, Pilate sent Him to Herod, commanding to enquire of him, that he might know for certain what he wanted to be done with Him, making Christ a convenient occasion of reconciliation with the king.

---

143 Psalm 89:38–45 (88:39–46 LXX).
144 Zechariah 13:7.
145 Matthew 26:31; cf. Mark 14:27.
146 "The Twelve Prophets" refers to the Minor Prophets.
147 Paraphrased from Hosea 10:6.

In Jeremiah He thus declares His death and descent into Hades,[148] saying, "And the Lord, the Holy One of Israel, remembered his dead, which aforetime fell asleep in the dust of the earth; and he went down unto them, to bring the tidings of his salvation, to deliver them."[149] In this place He also renders the reason for His death, for His descent into Hades was the salvation of those who had died.

And, again, concerning His cross Isaiah says, "I stretched out my hands all day to a people who resisted and opposed."[150] For this is an indication of the cross. Clearer still, David says, "For many dogs encircled me. A gathering of those doing evil surrounded me. They pierced my hands and feet."[151] And again He says, "My heart became like beeswax melting in the middle of my belly . . . all my bones were scattered."[152] And again He says, "Rescue my soul from the sword. . . . Nail my flesh. . . . A gathering of those doing evil surrounded me."[153] In these words He clearly signifies that He would be crucified. Moses says the same thing to the people, "And your life shall be hanging before your eyes, and you shall be afraid day and night, and you shall not have trust in your life."[154]

Again David says: "They perceived and gazed upon me. They distributed my garments among themselves, and they cast a lot for my clothing."[155] At His crucifixion the soldiers parted His garments according to their custom. The garments they parted by tearing, but for the vesture, because it was woven from the top and was not sewn, they cast lots, that whoever it fell to should take it.

---

148 Hades is the abode of the dead, both righteous and unrighteous, where the righteous are comforted and the wicked tormented (see Luke 16:19–31; Acts 2:27, 31). First Peter 3:18–20 says that Jesus "preached to the spirits in prison" after He had been killed.
149 An apocryphal quotation of uncertain origin. Justin Martyr also quotes it (*Dialogue* 72.4), saying that the Jews have removed it from Jeremiah. Perhaps some copies of Jeremiah, available to Justin and Irenaeus, included it.
150 Isaiah 65:2.
151 Psalm 22:16 (21:17 LXX).
152 Psalm 22:14 (21:15 LXX). Phrases here reversed.
153 A composite quotation of Psalm 22:20 (21:21 LXX), 119 (118 LXX):120, and 22:16 (21:17 LXX). The same composite appears in the earlier Christian writing *Epistle of Barnabas* (5:13).
154 Deuteronomy 28:66.
155 Psalm 22:17b–18 (21:18b–19 LXX). See John 19:24.

Again, Jeremiah the prophet says: "And they took the thirty pieces of silver, the price of him that was valued, whom they of the children of Israel did value; And gave them for the potter's field, as the Lord appointed me."[156] For Judas, being one of Christ's disciples, when he saw that the Jews desired to kill Him, agreed and covenanted with them, because he had been reproved by Him. He took the thirty lawful staters[157] and betrayed Christ to them. Then, repenting of what he had done, he gave the silver back to the rulers of the Jews and hanged himself. But they, thinking it would be wrong to put the money into their treasury because it was the price of blood, used it to buy the ground of a certain potter for the burial of strangers.

At His crucifixion, when He asked for a drink, they gave Him vinegar to drink mingled with gall. This was declared through David: "And they gave gall for my food, and they gave me vinegar for my drink."[158]

THE MESSIAH'S RESURRECTION

And that, being raised from the dead, He ascended into heaven, David says thus: "The chariots of God are ten thousand-fold, thousands of those flourishing. The Lord is among them in [Zion],[159] in the holy place. Having gone up to the high place, you took as prisoners a body of captives. You received gifts in a person."[160] This refers to the destruction of the rule of the apostate angels. He declares also the place where He was to ascend into heaven from the earth. For "the Lord," he says, went "up to the high place" from Zion. For near Jerusalem, on the mount which is called the Mount of Olives, after He had risen from the dead, He assembled His disciples, and expounded to them the things concerning the kingdom of heaven.

---

156 Quoted from Matthew 27:9–10. The closest parallel to this in our Old Testament is Zechariah 11:12–13; some elements are similar to Jeremiah 32:6–10 (39:6–10 LXX).

157 Staters are a monetary unit. Smith argued that this expression, confusing in the Armenian, was intended to refer to money lawful for use as Temple offerings.

158 Psalm 69:21 (68:22 LXX).

159 The LXX and the Armenian text of the *Proof* read "Sinai" here, but Irenaeus apparently read "Zion," as his subsequent exposition makes clear.

160 Psalm 68:17–18 (67:18–19 LXX). See also Ephesians 4:8.

They saw Him ascend, and they saw how the heavens opened and received Him.

And David again says: "Lift up the gates, those rulers of you. Lift eternal gates, and the King of glory will enter."[161] For the everlasting gates are the heavens. Since the Word descended invisibly to created things, He was not made known in His descent to them, but because the Word was made flesh, He was visible in His ascension. When the powers saw Him, the angels below cried out to those who were on the firmament: "Lift up the gates, those rulers of you. Lift eternal gates, and the King of glory will enter."[162] And when they marveled and said, "Who is this?" those who had already seen Him testified a second time: "The Lord of mighty powers, he is this King of glory!"[163]

Being raised from the dead and exalted at the Father's right hand, He awaits the time appointed by the Father for the judgment, when all enemies shall be put under Him. The enemies are all those who were found in apostasy—angels, archangels, powers, and thrones—who despised the truth. The prophet David himself says: "The Lord said to my Lord, 'Be seated at my right side until I set your enemies as a footstool for your feet.'"[164] That He ascended back to the place from where He had descended, David says, "From the top of the heavens is its going out, and its end is until the top of the heavens." Then he signifies his judgment: "And there is none who will be hidden from its heat."[165]

THE CALLING OF THE GENTILES

If the prophets prophesied that the Son of God was to appear upon the earth, and prophesied also where on the earth and how and in what manner He should appear, and all these prophecies the Lord fulfilled, our faith in Him is well-founded, and the tradition of the preaching is true—that is, the testimony of the apostles. Being sent

---

161 Psalm 24 (23 LXX):7, 9.
162 Ibid.
163 Psalm 24 (23 LXX):10.
164 Psalm 110 (109 LXX):1.
165 Psalm 19:6 (18:7 LXX).

out by the Lord, they preached in all the world the Son of God, who came to suffer, and endured to the destruction of death and the quickening of the flesh, so that He could put away mankind's enmity towards God, which is unrighteousness, and that we should obtain peace with Him, doing that which is pleasing to Him. This was declared by the prophets in the words, "How beautiful are the feet of them that preach the gospel of peace, and bring glad tidings of good things!"[166] And that they were to go forth from Judaea and from Jerusalem, to declare to us the word of God, which is the law for us, Isaiah says thus, "For a law will come out from Zion and a word of the Lord from Jerusalem."[167] And that in all the earth they were to preach, David says: "Into all the earth their voice went out, and their words into the ends of the inhabited world."[168]

Isaiah teaches that men were to be saved, not by the wordiness of the Law, but by the brevity of faith and love. "For he is completing and cutting short a word with righteousness, because God will perform a shortened word in the whole world."[169] Therefore the Apostle Paul says, "Love is the fulfilling of the law,"[170] for he who loves God has fulfilled the Law. Moreover, the Lord, when He was asked which commandment is the first [in importance], said, "Thou shalt love the Lord thy God with all thy heart, and with all thy soul, and with all thy mind. This is the first and great commandment. And the second is like unto it, Thou shalt love thy neighbour as thyself. On these two commandments hang all the law and the prophets."[171] So then by our faith in Him He has made our love to God and our neighbor to grow, making us godly, righteous, and good. And therefore "a shortened word" has God made "in the whole world."

---

166 Romans 10:15, quoting Isaiah 52:7 closer to the Masoretic Text reading than the Septuagint reading.
167 Isaiah 2:3b.
168 Psalm 19:4 (18:5 LXX); see also Romans 10:18.
169 Isaiah 10:22b–23 (modified from NETS LXX). See also Romans 9:28.
170 Romans 13:10b.
171 Matthew 22:37–40.

And that after His ascension He was to be exalted above all, and that there would be none to be compared and equaled unto Him, Isaiah says thus:

> Who is the one who judges me? Let him withstand me at once. Yes, who is the one who is justified? Let him approach the Son of God. . . . Look! You all will grow old like a garment, and a moth will devour you.[172]

In the end, those who serve God will be saved by His name. Isaiah says: "And a new name will be proclaimed over those who serve me, which will be praised upon the earth, for they will bless the true God."[173] And that this blessing He Himself would bring about, and would Himself redeem us by His own blood, Isaiah declared, saying, "Not an elder or a messenger but he himself has saved them, because he loved them and spared them. He himself ransomed them."[174]

Isaiah declared that He would not send the redeemed back to the legislation of Moses—for the Law was fulfilled in Christ—but would have them live in newness by the Word, through faith in the Son of God and love, saying:

> Do not call to mind the former things, and do not consider the ancient things. Look! I will do new things that will now spring forth, and you will perceive them, and I will make a way in the wilderness and rivers in the waterless place . . . to give my chosen race to drink, my people whom I have preserved, to tell of my magnificent acts.[175]

The called-out ones from the Gentiles were at first a "wilderness" and a "waterless place," for the Word had not passed through them, nor given them the Holy Spirit to drink. He fashioned the new "way" of godliness and righteousness, and made copious "rivers" to spring forth, sending the Holy Spirit over the earth,

---

172 Isaiah 50:8b–9. Modified from Lexham English Septuagint.
173 Isaiah 65:15b–16a.
174 Isaiah 63:9.
175 Isaiah 43:18–21.

as it had been promised through the prophets, that in the end of the days He should pour out the Spirit upon the face of the earth.

Therefore our calling is "in newness of spirit, and not in the oldness of the letter,"[176] even as Jeremiah prophesied:

> "Look! The days are coming," declares the Lord, "and I will establish a new covenant with the house of Israel and the house of Judah, not according to the covenant that I established with their fathers on the day I seized their hand to bring them out of the land of Egypt; for they did not remain in my covenant, and I neglected them," declares the Lord. "For this is my covenant that I will establish with the house of Israel after those days," declares the Lord. "In giving, I will give my laws into their mind, and I will write them upon their hearts. And I will become a God for them, and they will become a people for me. And each one will not teach his fellow citizen, or each his brother, saying, 'Know the Lord!' because everyone will know me, from the smallest of them to the greatest of them, because I will be gracious to their injustices. And I shall not remember their sins any longer."[177]

That the called-out ones from among the Gentiles would inherit these promises, to whom also the new covenant was opened up, Isaiah says: "This is what the Lord, the God of Israel, says: 'On that day a person will trust the one who made him, and his eyes will look to the Holy One of Israel. And they will certainly not trust the altars or in the works of their hands, which their fingers made.'"[178] This was very plainly said of people who have forsaken idols and believed in God our Maker through the Holy One of Israel. Christ is the Holy One of Israel, and He became visible to men, and to Him we look eagerly and behold Him. We trust not in altars, nor in the works of our hands.

And that He should become visible among us—for the Son of God became Son of man—and be found of us who before had no knowledge [of Him], the Word Himself says thus in Isaiah: "I became evident to those who did not consult me; I was found by those

---

176 Romans 7:6.
177 Jeremiah 31 (38 LXX):31–34. See also Hebrews 8:8–12.
178 Isaiah 17:6b–8a.

who did not seek me. I said, 'Look! Here I am,' to a people who have not called upon my name."[179]

That this race was to become a holy people was declared in the Twelve Prophets[180] by Hosea:

> I will call them my people, which were not my people; and her beloved, which was not beloved. And it shall come to pass, that in the place where it was said unto them, Ye are not my people; there shall they be called the children of the living God.[181]

This also was said by John the Baptist, "God is able of these stones to raise up children unto Abraham."[182] For our hearts, being withdrawn and taken away from the stony worship, behold God by means of faith and become sons of Abraham, who was justified by faith. Therefore God says by Ezekiel the prophet:

> And I will give them another heart and give them a new spirit and remove the stone heart from their flesh and give them a fleshly heart, in order that they may go in my duties and guard my ordinances and do them, and they will be my people, and I will be their God.[183]

So then by the new calling, the Gentiles experienced a change of heart through the Word of God, when He "was made flesh and dwelt" with men. His disciple John says, "And the Word was made flesh, and dwelt among us."[184] Wherefore the Church bears much fruit of the redeemed. No longer is Moses the mediator, nor Elijah the messenger, but the Lord Himself has redeemed us, granting many more children to the Church than to the first Synagogue. As Isaiah declared, "Rejoice, O barren one who does not bear."[185] The "barren one" is the Church, which never at all in former times presented sons to God. "Break forth, and shout, you who are not in labor! Because

---

179 Isaiah 65:1. See also Romans 10:20.
180 "The Twelve Prophets" refers to the Minor Prophets.
181 KJV. Irenaeus' quote matches the form of the prophecy quoted by Paul in Romans 9:25–26. See also Hosea 2:23, 1:10.
182 Matthew 3:9.
183 Ezekiel 11:19–20.
184 John 1:14a.
185 Isaiah 54:1a NETS LXX.

more are the children of the desolate woman than of her that has a husband."[186] Now the first Synagogue had the Law as a husband.

Moreover Moses in Deuteronomy says that the Gentiles should be "the head," and the unbelieving people "the tail."[187] And again he says:

> They made me jealous against what is not God; they irritated me with their idols, and I will make them jealous against what is not a nation; I will provoke them to wrath against a foolish nation.[188]

[This was] because they forsook the God who is, and worshiped and served the gods who are not, and killed the prophets of God, and "they prophesied through the Baal,"[189] who was the idol of the Canaanites. The Son of God, who is, they despised and condemned, but they chose [to save] Barabbas the robber, who had been taken for murder. The eternal King they disavowed, and they acknowledged as their king the temporal Caesar. It pleased God to grant their inheritance to the foolish Gentiles, even to those who were not under the rule of God and who did not know what God is. Since, then, by this calling life has been given to us, and God has summed up again for Himself in us the faith of Abraham, we ought not to turn back any more to the first legislation. For we have received the Lord of the Law, the Son of God, and by faith in Him we learn to love God with all our heart, and our neighbor as ourselves. The love of God is far from all sin, and love to the neighbor works no ill to the neighbor.[190]

Wherefore also we do not need the Law as a tutor. Behold, we speak with the Father, and we stand in His presence, being children in malice,[191] and grown strong in all righteousness and sobriety. For no longer shall the Law say, "You shall not commit adultery"[192] to him who has no desire at all for another's wife, nor, "You shall not

---

186 Isaiah 54:1b. See also Galatians 4:27.
187 Deuteronomy 28:44.
188 Deuteronomy 32:21. See also Romans 10:19.
189 Jeremiah 23:13b.
190 Romans 13:10.
191 See 1 Corinthians 14:20.
192 Exodus 20:14 (20:13 LXX).

murder"[193] to him who has put away from himself all anger and enmity. Nor does it say, "You shall not desire your neighbor's field or his ox or his beast of burden,"[194] to those who have no care at all for earthly things, but store up the heavenly fruits; nor "eye for eye, tooth for tooth"[195] to him who counts no man his enemy, but all men his neighbors, and therefore cannot stretch out his hand at all for vengeance. It will not require tithes of him who consecrates all his possessions to God, leaving father and mother and all his family, and following the Word of God. And there will be no command to remain idle for one day of rest, to him who perpetually keeps sabbath, that is to say, who serves God in the temple of God, which is man's body, and does righteousness every hour. "Because I want mercy," He says, "rather than sacrifice, and knowledge of God rather than whole burnt offerings."[196] "But the lawless person who sacrifices a calf for me is like one who slays a dog, and the one who offers fine flour is like one who offers swine's blood."[197] "And it will be that everyone, whoever invokes the name of the Lord, will be saved."[198]

There is "none other name" of the Lord "under heaven given among men, whereby we must be saved,"[199] except that of God, which is Jesus Christ the Son of God. Demons, evil spirits, and all apostate energies are subject by the invocation of the name of Jesus Christ, crucified under Pontius Pilate.

He is separated and withdrawn from among men, and yet there is a separation and division among mankind. Wherever any of those who believe on Him invoke and call upon Him and do His will, He is near and present, fulfilling the requests of those who call upon Him with pure hearts. Thus receiving salvation, we continually give thanks to God, who delivered us by His great, inscrutable, and unsearchable wisdom, and proclaimed the salvation from heaven—the

---

193 Exodus 20:13 (20:15 LXX).
194 Abbreviated from Exodus 20:17.
195 Exodus 21:24a. See Matthew 5:38ff.
196 Hosea 6:6. See Matthew 9:13, 12:7.
197 Isaiah 66:3a.
198 Joel 2:32.
199 Acts 4:12.

visible coming of our Lord, that is, His living as man—to which we by ourselves could not attain. "The things which are impossible with men are possible with God."[200] Wherefore also Jeremiah[201] says concerning her [wisdom]:[202]

> Who went up into heaven and took her and brought her down from the clouds? Who crossed over beyond the sea and discovered her and who will bring her for choicest gold? There is no one who knows her way or ponders her path. However, the one who comprehends everything knows her; he discovered her with his discernment. The one who created the earth into eternal time filled it with herds of four-footed animals. The one who sends the light and it goes, he summoned it and it obeyed him with trembling. And the stars twinkled brightly in their watches and were cheerful. He called them and they said, "We are here." They twinkled brightly with cheer for the one who made them. This is our God. No other can be compared with him. He discovered every path of knowledge and gave it to Jacob, his child, and to Israel, who was loved by him. After this she appeared upon the earth and lived among humans. This is the document of the commands of God, and the law that is exists into eternity. All who hold her are destined for life, but those who forsake her will perish.[203]

Now by "Jacob" and "Israel" he means the Son of God, who received power from the Father over our life, and after having received this power, brought it down to us who were far off from Him. He "appeared upon the earth and lived among humans," mingling and mixing the Spirit of God the Father with the creature formed by God, that man might be after the image and likeness of God.

THE PREACHING OF THE TRUTH

This, beloved, is the preaching of the truth, and this is the manner of our redemption. This is the way of life which the prophets proclaimed, Christ established, the apostles delivered, and the Church in all the world hands on to her children. This must we keep with all

200 Luke 18:27; see also Matthew 19:26; Mark 10:27.
201 The following quotation is from the book of Baruch, part of the Old Testament Apocrypha.
202 The early Christians understood Old Testament passages which personified Wisdom to be referring to the divine *Logos*/Word, Jesus Christ (for another example, see Proverbs 8). Wisdom is a feminine noun in both Greek and Hebrew, which is why it is referred to as a "she" in these passages and by Irenaeus.
203 Baruch 3:29–4:1.

certainty, with a sound will and pleasing to God, with good works and a right-willed disposition.

No one should think that God the Father is someone other than our Creator, as the heretics imagine.[204] They despise the God who is, and make gods of that which is not, and they fashion a Father of their own above our Creator, and imagine that they have found out for themselves something greater than the truth. All these are impious blasphemers against their Creator and against the Father, as we have shown in *Exposure and Overthrow of Knowledge Falsely So-called*.[205] Others reject the coming and incarnation of the Son of God,[206] which the apostles delivered and the prophets declared beforehand, even such as should be the summing up of mankind, as we have shown you in brief; these are also counted among those who lack faith. Others do not receive the gifts of the Holy Spirit, and cast away from themselves the prophetic grace,[207] by which water man bears the fruit of life unto God. These are they of whom Isaiah speaks: "For they will be," he says, "like a terebinth tree that has cast off its leaves, and like an orchard that does not have water."[208] These are in no way serviceable to God, since they cannot bear any fruit.

So then in respect of the three points of our seal,[209] error has strayed widely from the truth. Either they reject the Father, or they do not accept the Son and speak against His incarnation, or else they

---

204 Second-century heretical groups such as the Gnostics and the Marcionites maintained that the world was created by a being other than the Father of Jesus Christ. This being (called the Demiurge) was, according to their theology, the God of the Old Testament, who was ignorant, arrogant, and perhaps evil. Jesus came as the messenger of a higher God to deliver humans from the bondage of evil matter, which had been created by this lower power. The early Christians soundly refuted such errors, and Irenaeus himself wrote the voluminous *Against Heresies*, his other surviving work, to combat such ideas. By showing that the coming of Jesus had been prophesied in the Old Testament, the *Proof* also demonstrated the unity of the Old and New Testaments under one God, thus refuting Gnosticism.

205 Irenaeus' other surviving work, known today as *Against Heresies*.

206 Since they believed that matter (including the human body) was inherently evil and the product of the inferior Demiurge, Gnostics denied that Jesus Christ possessed a true human body.

207 Who Irenaeus is referring to with this criticism is uncertain, but he could be referring to the Marcionites, who rejected the Old Testament and, thus, the prophecies about Christ which it contained.

208 Isaiah 1:30.

209 This refers to confession of the three persons of the Trinity at baptism, which Irenaeus had earlier called "the seal of eternal life."

do not receive the Spirit, that is, they reject prophecy. Of all such we must beware, and shun their ways, if in very truth we desire to be well-pleasing to God and to attain the redemption that is from Him.

For other excellent titles on the historic Christian faith, contact:

Sermon on the Mount Publishing
P.O. Box 246
Manchester, MI 48158
(734) 428-0488
the-witness@sbcglobal.net
www.kingdomreading.com

Printed in the USA
CPSIA information can be obtained
at www.ICGtesting.com
LVHW020423091024
793327LV00012B/479